I AM

ABIGAIL

COMPELLING STORIES OF WOMEN WHO BROKE FREE FROM THE CYCLE OF ABUSE

LASHELLE ADAMS

I AM ABIGAIL

ISBN: 978-1-7327674-5-4

Library of Congress Control Number: 2018911745

Printed in USA by Vision to Fruition Publishing House

www.vision-fruition.com

Dedication

I dedicate this book to God first, it was You that kept my mind and strengthened my heart when I didn't want to go on.

To my daddy, Clinton Adams, since mom has been gone you have been my rock.

To my mom, Mattie Adams, the impact you made while on earth is priceless and I am the woman that I am today because of you.

To my son, my heart, Jordan, it's all because of you!

To my chief support system throughout my journey; Tish, Wendy, Shawn and Latia you are my lifetimers!

To all the women who are going through a difficult time in your own relationships, hang in there - your help is on the way.

Acknowledgments

Thank you to my Pastors, Wayne & Michelle Green, for carrying Jordan and me in your hearts. For always praying for us even when we left for a short while.

Thank you, Tameka Woodard, for your encouragement and my "DMV Wives" sisters. You believed in me and inspired me to stay when I wanted to quit!

Thank you, Margaret Banks and Mary Mannhardt for your wisdom, counsel and lending a helping hand.

To all the women who imparted in me and shared your personal testimony prompting me to write this book, Thank You!

Prologue

I Am Abigail is designed to be a quick read based on real life experiences. I wrote I Am Abigail to support those dealing with difficult companions who have issues such as: unstable personalities, control issues, irrational reasoning and uncontrollable anger. These short stories address questions that often torment an abused victims' mind such as "how can I help my partner?", "Do I go, or do I stay?", or "Lord is this Your will or mine?"

Though none of these women characterized are mental health experts or proclaim to have all the answers - what they do have is experience. They lived to tell their stories and vowed that they would not keep it to themselves. Each character struggled to reveal their testimonies, and all had one undeniable thing in common - that is to prevent others from taking their path and making wise decisions in advance. The goal is to help other victims in any way possible.

So many women are manipulated and hide in shame when they become victims of abuse. It really doesn't matter who you are, anyone can be confronted with it – the wives of ministers, entrepreneurs, stay-at-home moms and even teenagers in relationships.

It took courage to come forth with this book not because I wanted to, but because I had too. I do hope that you will enjoy this short yet uplifting book and apply it to your own relationship where or if necessary.

You're Not Crazy

Abuse comes in all types of the packages and regardless of how it is delivered, it's still Abuse. To be mishandled, mistreated or misused are just a few adjectives that describe the cruel act of abuse. In order to recognize if your relationship is healthy, unhealthy or even abusive you must first be able to identify it. Some of the following stories may be relatable to you in helping you identify your situation and assist you with any dilemmas.

Abuse is a complex concept, it is easily defined and yet very difficult to understand and identify.

Generally, people don't recognize or even suspect silent abusers such as emotional or mental until they have experienced it or someone that they love has. These types of misleading yet subtle abuses can interrupt your day to day routines such as work performance or nurturing of children and eventually robbing one of a healthy life. When it's your mother, sister, friend or even brother, it becomes real to you!

Consequently, and overtime domestic violence has awakened our world through broken families, tumultuous violence, psychological breakdowns, and even death.

4

Historically and especially in Christendom, one was persuaded by their pastors, parents or traditionalists to stick with their spouse no matter what! When one was dependent on their spouse, afraid or desired to please the Lord according to scripture, they become enslaved into bondage.

God's word always confirms and thankfully He left a blueprint for those that choose to adhere to it. It's wise to seek counsel and opinion from those who are qualified but above all, consult with God! A very clear description pertaining to identifying an abusive marriage is found in Ephesians 5:28-29 where it says, *"So ought men to love their wives as their own bodies. He that loveth his wife loveth himself.* *29 For no man ever yet hated his own flesh; but nourisheth and cherisheth it, even as the Lord the church."* Though this scripture does not necessarily mandate separation, you must pray for guidance according to your situation and your husbands' heart.

Don't get caught up in worry with separation leading to a divorce but be more concerned about your today and let God handle your tomorrow. Fear will prohibit you from moving forward with what is best for your marriage and trusting God with the unknowns. We understand that God hates divorce and it is his will that we experience the joys of marriage. So, if you are married and experiencing any form of abuse you can still believe God for deliverance in your husbands' heart, but you must proceed with patience, caution, prayer, and wisdom. Keep your heart clean towards your spouse and be assured that things will work together for your good!

Beloved at this moment your safety and sanity is what matters, all else will follow!

To those who are dating or engaged: if it doesn't feel right, if it seems awkward or your partner is just confusing, follow the signs. Phrases such as "It's not that serious", "You're too emotional" or "You're a drama queen" may come to mind if they are condescending, but warning: these thoughts are not to be taken lightly. If they shut down on you in pre-marriage, they will shut you out post-marriage. I want you to know that you're not irrational in your thinking, **YOU'RE NOT CRAZY!**

Blurred Lines

Identifying Types of Abuse

A buse is a touchy subject and sensitive matter that can be very fuzzy and complex at times. Emotional, verbal, mental, psychological and even spiritual abuse are all hard to prove and very hard to escape. Below are some simple definitions that could help you identify these types of abuse.

Although psychological abuse is not as evident as physical, the wounds go very deep!

Physical abuse

This is the most common and clear abuse. It is physical touch that shows aggression, hurts or harms. One should seek immediate help and get a safe place to stay. Many people are killed as a result of this kind of abuse.

Psychological abuse

This is tricky or vague to identify. It deals with the mental state. There are also lots of mind games and it is very similar to mental, emotional or verbal abuse; it can eventually lead to physical abuse.

Verbal abuse

This kind of abuse is clear but tricky to identify. It involves verbally saying ugly things about or to a person. It comes with belittling, downsizing and condescending comments; and it messes with the mental state and esteem of the person who is abused. When someone women are verbally abused for too long, they no longer see anything good in themselves and they can't see anything right or beautiful about themselves.

Spiritual abuse

This can be very fuzzy or tricky to identify. The abusers in this case are occult religions or leaders that are viewed as God by parishioners. These people (the abusers) use Bible scriptures to manipulate the mind of the abused.

Emotional abuse

This kind of abuse can be very vague and hard to identify. It is a deliberate action intended to crush one's heart or spirit, while playing with the emotions and mind. There is a denial of the right to express your feelings without being criticized.

A Funny Foundation

Y ou've heard the term a firm foundation and its importance. When something is firm in the natural, its solid, unyielding, and the roots are strong. In the spirit realm, if the foundation isn't planted with deep roots, it could deprive you of your best life emotionally, financially and relationally.

There is a saying "What you may laugh at now you will cry for later". This means that you shouldn't ignore foolish actions or silly gestures by passing them off as being a simple joke or assuming that it is just a simple personality. If they can never be serious and it's all about fun and games, then it's a funny foundation. When a disagreement or misunderstanding goes from a storm to a tsunami that is a very rocky foundation. If things are always difficult and roadblocks are constantly up it's not firm but it's funny, a very amusing foundation that can turn out like that of a circus show!

"Therefore everyone who hears these words of mine and puts them into practice is like a wise man who built his house on the rock. 25 The rain came down, the streams rose, and the winds

blew and beat against that house; yet it did not fall, because it had its foundation on the rock. 26 But everyone who hears these words of mine and does not put them into practice is like a foolish man who built his house on sand. 27 The rain came down, the streams rose, and the winds blew and beat against that house, and it fell with a great crash."

Matthew 7:24-27

It's important to have balance in every aspect from laughter to crying, sickness or health, financially stripped or abundance; however it is only when each is tested that there is the proof of foundation. Regardless of the type of relationship such as a husband and wife, parent and child, or even business, the groundwork must be established from the very start. Essentially there should be friendship, authenticity, loyalty, open communication and Christ as the center to yield a firm footing.

"For everything there is a season, a time for every activity under heaven.2 A time to be born and a time to die. A time to plant and a time to harvest. A time to kill and a time to heal. A time to tear down and a time to build up.4 A time to cry and a time to laugh a time for every activity under heaven."
Ecclesiastes 3:1-4

Pearls of Wisdom

It's important to be who you are from the very beginning of your dating process. Be sure that there are no hidden secrets or underlying issues that will arise later and pay attention to your partner if they are truly being themselves. If you not only love but like who they are as a person, then that is a good indication of their character. Go and be blessed but above all make sure that you have a Firm Foundation!

Abigail

"A Wise Woman"

I n the Bible, the book of First Samuel chapter 25 tells the story of an astonishingly attractive and intelligent woman named Abigail meaning the source of joy who had a rich husband named Nabal meaning fool.

"Now the name of the man was Nabal, and the name of his wife Abigail. The woman was discerning and beautiful, but the man was harsh and badly behaved; he was a Calebite."

First Samuel 25:3

This story is so compelling because Abigail was an example of a woman who loved her family, defended her husband and had a personal relationship with God. Undoubtedly, today Abagail would be termed as a boss chick because she was quick on her feet and about her business. Like some of the women in the forthcoming chapters, Abigail knew the temperament of her husband, but she also knew how to pray and intercede.

King David simply sent his men to extend to Nabal a message of peace pertaining to the upcoming festivities in the land and that all would be well. Nabal was so arrogantly caught up with his riches and out of touch with reality that he responded with a rude reply. Nabal didn't realize who he was messing with and that he offended David, therefore bringing calamity to his house. As David and his men strapped up for war, God sent Abigail a messenger to warn her of the danger in route.

"And Abigail came to Nabal, and behold, he was holding a feast in his house, like the feast of a king. And Nabal's heart was merry within him, for he was very drunk. So, she told him nothing at all until the morning light. ³⁷ In the morning, when the wine had gone out of Nabal, his wife told him these things, and his heart died within him, and he became as a stone. ³⁸ And about ten days later the LORD struck Nabal, and he died."

First Samuel 25:36-38

Abigail not only intervened in the spiritual realm but also in the natural realm! She gathered a peace offering such as fine foods and wine and met them on their route. I believe that Abigail was beautifully adorned when she greeted David and obviously, she was spiritually led by what words to say and how she conveyed them. The result was that she prevented her entire household from being destroyed and rich inheritance from dying. Sadly, her husband Nabal was so calloused that when he heard of what his wife had done on his behalf, his heart grew sick and within ten days he was gone. Soon thereafter, David sent for Abigail to be his wife.

Women, we want to be like Abigail because she thought before she reacted. We have all missed the mark before but now is a great time to start and learn from her response. Had she been defensive, her entire household would have died, and she would have never had a second chance.

Lessons to learn from Abigail

Be careful with your choices. Abigail means source of joy but Nabal means fool. What is the connection between fool and joy?

Absolutely nothing!

What choices are you making concerning your life and your partner that will put you in a position of peril in the future? The bible says there is no relationship between light and darkness. You are the light beloved! *"Submit yourselves, then, to God. Resist the devil, and he will flee from you". James 4:7*

Abigail was an intelligent God-fearing woman who obviously used her tongue as a weapon and defense against the enemy. The enemy that wanted to abort her entire destiny. James 1:5 says "If anyone lacks wisdom let him . ask God who gives generously without finding fault and it will be given to such a person". Ask God for wisdom today. God wouldn't look at your misdeeds and say I wouldn't give her wisdom because of all the things she did wrong. You only need to believe and then it is settled.

In an instant God changed her story and Abigail was upgraded from widow to Queen. I'm not sure if Nabal already possessed bad character and an ugly heart or not when

Abigail married him. What matters is that her heart was right and towards God. If you made a mistake in the product of your decision for a mate, understand things are working together for your good. Be encouraged with Abigail's testimony for God has no respect of persons!

Virtue, Beauty, and Wisdom granted Abigail Favor!

Thoughts | Reflections | Notes

_____

_____

_____

_____

_____

_____

_____

_____

_____

_____

_____

_____

_____

_____

_____

_____

_____

_____

_____

_____

_____

_____

Samantha

"Own It"

A major step to freedom and deliverance is being true to thyself. So often we want to place the blame on others for our misfortunes, but sometimes we must point the fingers back to ourselves. If you are in a dominating, controlling or abusive relationship of any form you must reflect and go back to your beginning. You will recall **there was a sign or something that showed you that all wasn't right, if only you inclined your heart to that thought or warning.** You're probably thinking but it wasn't my fault and perhaps it wasn't. I need you to understand that is not point! Realize, recognize and own your contribution to the furtherance of entering an unhealthy situation.

"When someone shows you who they are believe them; the first time."

Maya Angelou

The best thing Samantha could have done to prevent her former husband and herself from future heartache was postponing the wedding until the appropriate time, but she let commitment interfere. **Samantha spared her husband to be, family, and friends' temporary**

disappointment but she suffered years of emotional agony and pain.

Samantha had to acknowledge that when her fiancé' gave her the silent treatment or was overly aggressive that those were red flags. Instead of allowing the Abigail inside of her to stand up with boldness, she succumbed to her fiancé's controlling ways. Just simply saying "Yes, I love you, but you have a problem and I cannot marry you until your anger is addressed! You must handle your offenses differently" would have made a major difference. Either he would have agreed to get the help, or the wedding would have been called off, plain and simple! Naively, she told herself a lie (not the devil) that because she loved God and he loved her that his unkind ways would somehow subside, and things would get better.

After her divorce, Samantha began to speak out more about her marital experiences because she knew that by sharing what she endured, it would set others free. Each time she would speak, she humbly began with "This is not a badge on my ex-husband but rather about setting other women free and if exposing me will do that then here I am". The fact of the matter was that as bad as she was mistreated, she had to accept her own liabilities within the marriage because God had already exposed his heart. It was on Samantha to see it for what it was and own up to it!

If anyone thinks they are something when they are not, they deceive themselves. Each one should test their own actions. Then they can take pride in themselves alone, without comparing themselves to someone else.

It's not about what you didn't know but what you are aware of.

Pearls of Wisdom

If you're dating and experiencing any form of control, aggression or mistreatment now is the time to address it. Trust God for the strength and boldness as he will guide you on how to approach the matter. Be clear to your partner and true to yourself about your feelings and if they are not willing to adhere, spare yourself the grief and end it now. Ladies, now you are on the path to true healing and who God really has for you.

Lessons to learn from Samantha

When you point a finger forward three others are pointing back at you. Acknowledging your own wrong and accepting your responsibility is a recipe for healing. This is not the same thing as wallowing in blame guilt or self-pity. *"There is therefore now no condemnation to those who are in Christ Jesus" Romans 8:1.* We have the blood of Jesus that washes our consciousness from guilt. Consequently, this can prevent you from a cycle of mistakes in the future and help others to dodge some abusive bullets if possible!

Accepting wrongdoing while you are single and disapproving of it when you are married is hypocrisy! What standards have you set, or limits do you have? If you haven't yet, now is a great time. So please Be true to thyself!

Thoughts | Reflections | Notes

_____
_____
_____
_____
_____
_____
_____
_____
_____
_____
_____
_____
_____
_____
_____
_____
_____
_____
_____
_____
_____
_____
_____
_____
_____

Patrice

"Take Your Personal Advice"

P atrice was in her early forties when she got married, she was a mature Christian and so deemed herself as rather wise. After all, she had given advice to so many others guiding them in the right direction and most of them are still together till this very day. She had made enough mistakes (so she thought) that surely, she was making an intelligent decision to marry Mike. However, during the courtship, there were days and weeks of the silent treatment which left Patrice hurt and confused with perplexed thoughts of trying to figure out the man she would soon unite within Holy matrimony.

"But when he, the Spirit of truth, comes, he will guide you into all the truth. He will not speak on his own; he will speak only what he hears, and he will tell you what is yet to come."

John 16:13

Unfortunately, Patrice had guided others better than herself because she had graciously adjusted to look beyond Mike's offenses by covering them up or simply not facing reality. She soon realized that what may have worked for others in their marriage would not benefit her own. Every couple, each union and the structure of every man was different. When weighing the pros vs cons, the good and the bad, they always appear to favor the lesser in pre-marriage but often post marriage things become heightened.

"Never apologize for trusting your intuition – your brain can play tricks, your heart can be blind, but your gut is always right."

Rachel Wolchin

Often, we give a lending ear to others and respond with great feedback especially in relation to the Word of God, but we forget that we must use that same instruction we receive for ourselves. If only she would have believed in her own wisdom, perhaps she could have avoided the inevitable. Superstitious people may refer to it as our gut feeling, the well-educated may term it as intuition and spiritual believers would call it Holy-Spirit. It is my opinion, that they all are a gift from God to guide us in the right direction.

[11] *For I know the plans and thoughts that I have for you,' says the LORD, 'plans for peace and well-being and not for disaster, to give you a future and a hope."*

Jeremiah 29:11 (AMP)

Pearls of Wisdom

Are you presently dating or engaged? If so, this is a great time to do some inward examination of yourself and your partner. Pray, be still and listen to what the Spirit has to say! ***Don't be afraid to swallow a hard pill and eat some humble pie by receiving your own advice.*** If you have concerns or detect flaws it doesn't necessarily indicate ending your relationship. You are in the best position and now is the time to address all issues, if any at all. If you are in fear or cannot speak your truth without them exploding, now is a good time to walk away!

Remember if you have desires for your partner and want to see a change you must also be willing to change*

Lessons to learn from Patrice

"Practice what you Preach" a cliché that is easier said than done. Not only must we walk the walk but talk the talk and put our own counsel into practice.

If what you know doesn't work for you then maybe, consider the advice you have given in the past must be adjusted. Have you tried it or is it easier said than done? Generally, our personality, thought process and belief will determine what will work in our relationships.

Always remain humble. If no one can talk to you, or address your flaws because you are high minded and prideful please check that now. Ask God to teach you to draw the line within because he doesn't dwell where there is arrogance.

The goal is to survive, thrive and be a light for other people who have the same challenge. Give wise counsel and receive guidance for yourself as well. *"Where there is no guidance the people fall, But in abundance of counselors there is victory". Proverbs 11:14*

Thoughts | Reflections | Notes

Sarah

"The Side Eye"

T he first few years of marriage were a constant rollercoaster of verbal and mental torment for Sarah. She was overwhelmed with sorrow and felt she couldn't take it anymore. There were countless unkind deeds along with threatening words from her husband to get out of the home. One day, she thought I'm going to do just that she returned their marriage certificate, his ring and a sticky note with scripture and left it resting on the pillow. She finally said enough was enough! She called her sister and they proceeded to move her things and pick up her child from school for early dismissal.

"Red flags are moments of hesitation that determine our destination."

Mandy Hale, Th

When Sarah went to check out young Katlen from the school office, she was confronted by the lead secretary. As they sat on the couch together to fill out paperwork, under the secretary's voice she whispered: "Is it Mr.Thomas?" Initially, Sarah gave the side eye and thought about why the secretary was asking about her husband. Sarah had been introduced to the secretary before through her husband because she also lived in their neighborhood, but she had no idea until then that they had attempted to date prior to marriage. The secretary stated that "Mr. Thomas had invited her over and he was very domineering and aggressive. She never returned because she didn't feel a good vibe". Sarah felt embarrassed, hurt and angry at the same time. She was at a loss for words because she knew her husband and though she really loved him, deep down inside she knew it was true. Sadly, this was the confirmation of who he was and that she was making a very tough but accurate decision by removing herself and her child from the situation. Sarah knew then, that unless he was willing to get help with his issues and surrender to God she could not return. Sadly, they would never be happy, and life would be a living hell!

After fervent prayer, a candid conversation with her husband and professional Christian counseling together, there was no change. The Psychologist had cautioned her from the wealth of experience that the psychologist had *that a person who needs to control others, is not in control of himself.* He told her that he had once been that same husband and until he submitted to God there was no transformation and change from within. He couldn't be the husband that his wife needed.

Sarah knew that her husband was very angry, and he was aching inside. She also knew that he wasn't born that way but it was an indication of something deeper. She felt his pain and understood that people who are hurting, would also hurt other people. She believed God and refused to give up on her marriage, so in a cry of desperation, she boldly called her mother-in-law in hope that she could reach her son and maybe even have a family intervention. Sarah knew this was risky because her husband was a very private man and was firm about keeping any and everyone out of their business. She asked his mother, "Is there something from his childhood or learned behavior from his father that I should know about?" Astonishingly, her mother-in-law stated "There was nothing she could do because she had tried before to correct him, but he turned against her. She had finally won him back and she just couldn't risk losing her son again so she was going to back off the situation" Mr. Thomas had such a bad attitude at times and was known for holding grudges or giving the silent treatment for days to weeks at a time and no one was off limits. Not even the one who birthed him in the world, his mother could stop him hold grudges or keeping malice with people.

Sarah remembered her counselor's advice according to the knowledge of scripture, expertise, and wisdom that anyone can change and be delivered from being an abuser, but they had to acknowledge and want it. He told her "it was her choice", as any professional psychologist would do. However, he had warned her of these strong silent abusers and their ability to intensify if not dealt with.

"But Lot's wife looked back, and she became a pillar of salt."
Genesis 19:26

Sarah was prepared to walk hand in hand with her husband toward his healing and deliverance. She would do anything to save her marriage, so there was no choice but to stay put and stand firm until directed otherwise. Ultimately,

31

Mr. Thomas had to make some uncomfortable yet critical decisions that would benefit him personally and his entire family. However, the choice was up to him.

Pearls of Wisdom

Sarah's story was a bit complicated but understand that sometimes a therapeutic separation is necessary for a sane mind. Notice it never told you her outcome because I want to provoke your thinking and expand your thoughts! What would you have done? Did she leave pre-maturely or did she make the best decision? Every situation is a case by case scenario and everyone has a measure for their breaking point.

Lessons to learn from Sarah

Sarah wasn't rash in her decision, but she considered the whole matter before you her running out on the marriage. It was imperative that she understood there really was no choice but to leave if Mr. Thomas was not willing to deal with his demons. Sarah understood this was not her task to sort through or figure out. It was her job to be prayerful, patient, aware of her surroundings and to guard her safety. As much as she desired your husband to change, she could not get in the way of this process.

While dating or courting, get familiar with their family and friends. Especially his father, uncles, brothers and closest counterparts. Take note of their behavior or patterns; do they drink alcohol heavily or constantly? Are they rude or short with their own wives? Are they arrogant? Honestly answer these questions because this is a pretty close observation of how he will treat you.

Thoughts | Reflections | Notes

_____

_____

_____

_____

_____

_____

_____

_____

_____

_____

_____

_____

_____

_____

_____

_____

_____

_____

_____

_____

Tina

"The Fights Is On"

J ohn and Tina had a wonderful courtship, they agreed on practicing celibacy and not to live together until marriage. Tina was saved as a young adult but later had a child out of wedlock. That was a critical lesson which rededicated her life back to God and vowing to live according to the bible. John grew up a conservative Christian; his father was a Preacher and he attended church every Sunday as a child. He would tell her the lasting memories of how he would carry his father's bible assisting him in every way, even when it was things he didn't care to witness. John's mother was long divorced from his father and the reason was never told, which tormented John over the years. When they had family gatherings the mention of her deceased ex-husband was not even a whisper.

Newly married, Tina often wondered about a very peculiar tattoo that was painted on John's body and what it symbolized. Also, there were some collectibles around the house such as dead reptiles in jars, porcelain dragons, and prints of other Gods. Some of these items were given by friends as gifts in lieu of custom beliefs and he felt was an insult to return to them. The other things were collected as he spent his time overseas during his military tour. Initially, they battled over their view about the items, but Tina was convicted and decided to change her approach to John. Through loving words and a gentle tone, Tina was able to convince John to discard a few collectibles, although he wasn't happy with the decision. Tina was fervent in prayer because she knew that she was up against some demonic warfare and had hopes that after decluttering the home of some of this wicked paraphernalia, John would become knowledgeable about the importance of not entertaining evil forces in any way.

Tina soon found out that John was more religious and traditional than anything else. He had no relationship with Jesus Christ as his personal Savior.

The fall season had begun, trees were coloring beautiful hues of orange, reds, and greens and things were looking up until Halloween approached. This was a topic they never discussed in detail; Tina had made negligent assumptions about their practices during this pagan holiday season simply because they were both Christians. Her son was still a boy when they married, and they were merging their families by staying in the same house along with their own kids. One thing that Tina was never willing to compromise and extremely overprotective of was her child's soul and spiritual development. In prior years she would let him attend church events, family gatherings or take him walking herself for candy in lieu of Halloween. When they moved in with John, unbeknownst to her there were some Halloween decorations around the house she was not aware of. Skeleton heads, graveyard plots, ghosts and even a man-sized demon that was ever so scary! It blended well with the themed family-oriented neighborhood, but it was way too much for Tina to consume. They clashed like two rams in a tussle because of this and Tina felt this was unacceptable. She was fed up!

"For the weapons of our warfare are not of the flesh but have divine power to destroy strongholds."

Second Corinthians 10:4

Sleepless nights filled with prayer, constant fasting, and declaring of God's word over her husband's mind, heart, and soul. It seemed that things appeared worse before they became better and the first year of marriage was like being in full-time combat! Tina knew her husband possessed some serious mental and emotional issues that would often cause him to shut down and isolate himself. Through prayer, God had revealed to her that John had deep hurt and hidden secrets from the past and that he'd been spiritually abused as a child from his own father. Other matters were embedded through his stern military training and encounter with witchcraft spirits. ***If you're an intellectual thinker, to you the spiritual aspect of this may be a bit far-fetched, but I'm telling you that Demonic strongholds and generational curses are real.*** We have the authority through the holy-spirit to break the chains of bondage and tell them where to go!

Tina was hungry! She was hungry for God and to do his work, hungry to see her entire family saved and her husband delivered. Because of her endurance to fight during this battle and John's heart was no longer calloused but willing to surrender, he was set free and filled with the holy spirit. By

God's grace, the spirit of Abigail stood up in Tina, preventing a divorce from taking place and her household from collapsing.

Pearls of Wisdom

Fortunately, this story has a happy ending that didn't come with ease but a fight. Not only was Tina an active participant but so was John by humbling himself. Tina had no regrets for dating the Christian way, but she realized the approach could have been done much differently. Because of their distant relationship, she didn't visit often or as long as she could have. Tina's determination to live right before God prevented her from checking the sources for the man she was soon to marry, for one should never be so spiritually naïve that you don't practice wisdom!

"Don't be so heavenly minded that you're no earthly good!"

**If you're currently dating and considering marriage or engaged, be sure to check the sources. **

Lessons to learn from Tina

As much as you want to prevent temptation, you can date the Christian way without moving into the house of your fiancée. You can visit your fiancée with a trusted friend or speak with his pastor, friends and family. This will give you some of his spiritual inclination and character. Setting a time of prayer, fasting and bible study together would also be helpful. These are wonderful patterns that if you start them now, they will continue in the marriage. Remember your foundation is critical! Therefore, be bold as Abigail and stand your ground by putting up a banner for the Lord in your home.

I love how Tina stood her own ground to create a spiritual environment that allowed her child to believe in God and not in religion. We teach our children by being living examples for them. If Tina had not, her child could have fallen into false religion or other pagan practices. Let your children see God in you both in words and deed.

We must fight and choose our battles wisely by ultimately understanding that the battle does not belong to us but for the Lord to fix it. *"This is what the LORD says to you: 'Do not be afraid or discouraged because of this vast army. For the battle is not yours, but God's".* 2 Chronicles 20:15

Thoughts | Reflections | Notes

_____

_____

_____

_____

_____

_____

_____

_____

_____

_____

_____

_____

_____

_____

_____

_____

_____

_____

_____

_____

_____

_____

Cindy

"The Essence of Nature"

By nature, Cindy was soft-spoken, an introvert and often related to as meek in spirit by others. Cindy tried to see the good in everyone and didn't have room for negative space in her life. Her optimistic view of life's issues, faith in God and family was her motivation to keep going. Unlike some women, Cindy had no issues with Ephesians 5:22, which says, *"Wives, submit to your own husbands as unto the Lord."* Therefore, she didn't think it was strange when her husband asked during their courtship if she had an issue with submission or obedience. She told him she was going to be a submissive wife and it didn't lead to any argument or fight.

Cindy loved all God's creation and would often result in his nature for stillness and to hear from God. She looked forward to the sound of birds chirping in the morning or watching the deer prance through her backyard, visiting parks, walking trails, or just sitting by the pond for meditation and prayer.

But ask the animals, and they will teach you, or the birds in the sky and they will tell you; or speak to the earth, and it will teach you, or let the fish in the sea inform you. Which of all these does not know that the hand of the LORD has done this?

In his hand is the life of every creature and the breath of all mankind.

Job 12: 7-10

Everything was smooth right from their courtship until their wedding day. After that it became a night of sleepless rest and agonizing thoughts because her husband of just over two months was furious with her, what was supposed to be a joyous occasion turned into a nightmare! They had received an invitation to attend the lavish wedding of Cindy's longtime friend months ago and were excited about their weekend getaway as honeymooners themselves. They held hands and talked as Cindy enjoyed the beautiful view of blue skies and oceans filled with yachts while Frank drove. Finally, they arrived at the hotel, checked in their room, made love, took naps and before you knew it, it was time to get to the wedding. The tears wouldn't stop falling from Cindy's eyes as she and her husband witnessed the nuptials of another loving couple. Afterward, they left the church to head towards the 400-person reception. Parking and getting seated was a big ordeal but was worth it because the reception hall was elegantly decorated and the epitome of class.

While they were dating, Cindy had started preparing her new husbands' plates. Most of the time, it was a delight to Cindy to serve Frank and besides having his plate fixed was most preferred as well. At the party, the food was set up buffet style and with 400 people to feed you can only imagine what the line looked like. When their table was called, they both got up and grabbed their plates, however instead of him

42

just picking up his own food, he held out his plate for Cindy. Although it would have made things much easier and convenient to do his own, he still looked to Cindy to serve him. Frank happened to be allergic to seafood and on that night chicken and fish were on the buffet. By accident, Cindy placed fish on his plate and he blew up instantly with anger. He firmly grabbed her arm and commented that "She was trying to kill him and did she just want him to go and die?" She politely apologized and asked him to please tone it down in front of the other guests, but he continued to blame her to the point of no return. He retreated to the bar for a cocktail which heightened his anger and the night ended sour, silent and sad.

A quick-tempered man acts foolishly, and a man of evil devices is hated.

Proverbs 14:7

Frank could go from hot to cold or A to Z in seconds and being in a public setting or standing in front of the crowd was not exempt. Although they were newlyweds, this was not uncommon as it had intensified since marriage. Cindy was hoping for a peaceful weekend getaway filled with romance but what she feared most, became a reality.

The following morning as her husband lay asleep, Cindy remembered the cute little pond filled with ducks adjacent to the hotel. She decided to get dressed and head to the pond for solace and to commune with God about what took place the night before. Of course, Cindy couldn't wrap her head around the situation as she often wondered how her husband processed his thoughts or what made his mind tick? She was very concerned about his mental state and sincerely believed that medicine would help calm his nerves. She also knew that he had matters of the heart that needed to be addressed.

Charge it to his head or his heart, regardless, they both needed to be transformed.

Cindy asked God to prepare her for the conversation to come because if Frank hadn't humbled himself, once again, he would try to convince her that his actions were her fault. Franks' controlling ways were used to his wife's calm demeanor and closed mouth, but what he didn't know was that God was raising up an Abigail in her!

He that dwelleth in the secret place of the most High shall abide under the shadow of the Almighty.

Psalm 91:1

Pearls of Wisdom

Cindy had found her secret place and knew where to go to regain strength. Cindy couldn't help her God-given quiet personality, but she could decide that no longer would she be bullied or silent. Assumptions are often made about those who are meek in spirit as being pushovers, but everyone has a line that must be drawn. When an introverted person constantly deals with a controlling or difficult individual, it's imperative that they have an outlet because it's easier for a nervous breakdown to occur. If you haven't already, I challenge you to find a point of reference for peaceful solitude and to discover your secret place today!

Lessons to learn from Cindy

Becoming a believer in Jesus Christ is not enough reason for you to remain naive. As a kingdom believer you still will be confronted with struggle, challenges and life's disappointments. Don't be ignorant with the devil's devices by thinking that everyone thinks as you do. Cindy didn't know that when her husband asked if she was submissive, he was asking for his own selfish reasons and not as to the Lord.

By nature, Cindy was easily given into fear because of her personality. If this is your DNA now is a good time to denounce and break the chains of intimidation and anxiety off your life. Don't be afraid to ask questions but be bold even as Abigail was! This is not to cause an argument or make a point but a reason for you to be clear on any issue. It removes doubts or assumptions that are often created in our minds prematurely.

As you spend time in his presence, God will download you with wisdom and gird you with strength to do what once seemed impossible. Run after him with all that you have!

Thoughts |Reflections|

Notes

_____
_____
_____
_____
_____
_____
_____
_____
_____
_____
_____
_____
_____
_____
_____
_____
_____
_____
_____
_____
_____
_____

Gabrielle

"Not My Child"

I n the Thomas household structure, everything was always in order, cleanliness was standard living and nothing less was acceptable. The kids were taught to do an about-face upon rising in the morning to make up their beds. All the lights and televisions were immediately turned off when exiting a room. If dishes were left in the sink there would be hell to pay and for Heavens' sake, don't say one thing and do another or you'd have to drop to the floor and do a quick fifty. By fifty, I mean fifty push-ups and nothing less than this. No one was exempt, from Mrs. Thomas to the youngest child. The Thomas' ran a tight ship, and everyone knew this and fell in line!

Gabrielle was a stay at home mom and did the majority of managing the kids when it came to school, sports and church activities. She and Don were married for over eighteen years and had five children ages 17, 13, 10 and 8-year-old twins. Although Gabrielle respected her husband as head of household and an awesome provider, she wasn't always in agreement with his method of discipline toward the kids. Don was a very hard-working professional with a stern background and no excuse type of mentality. He was extremely hard on himself both physically with his daily workouts and his materialistic statuses such as the cars he drove and the home he lived in. Although he meant well, he could only help but be firm with his wife and children which often resulted in emotional, verbal and psychological abuse.

Earlier during the marriage, they attended church regularly until Don was offended by clergy and because he was a no-nonsense type of guy, and he had completely stopped going to Church. Unfortunately, this changed his perception of born again christians and deception crept into his thoughts, poisoning his mind against the importance of church attendance. Soon he wanted to control everything, even where and when the family went to worship. He had even decided to teach his kids the bible and they didn't have to attend church against the desire of his wife.

And let us not neglect our meeting together, as some people do, but encourage one another, especially now that the day of his return is drawing near.

Hebrews 10:25

Gabrielle knew that he wasn't equipped nor in position to hold bible study for the children because his heart had turned into stone. She knew this would be very dangerous for her kids and though she had no control over him, she stood her ground (in a loving way) and kept taking her children. Although he didn't like it, God humbled him and shut his mouth concerning the church.

Occasionally, Don would try to demote Gabrielle to that of a child rather than treating her as a wife. She didn't realize it, but she had become immune to his condescending ways.

Although Gabrielle and the older children seemed to have a handle on Mr. Thomas's rigid ways, the youngest kids had a difficult time adapting to his systems and routines. The twins were of a different breed and unlike their older siblings, they were both outspoken and they lived their lives by speaking up when they were not in agreement with whatever was going on. Part of the blame was instilled in them by their father to never back down and to stand up like a man. After all, they were his only boys so by the age of seven they were in training for yard maintenance such as grass cutting, weed pulling, tree trimming, and snow shoveling. The rest was credited to their God-given Choleric type personalities which are known for being adventurous, determined, candid, competitive, and strong-willed. Essentially, they were fun-loving kids who looked forward to attending children's church and bible study mostly with mom and their sisters. When you meet the twins you couldn't deny that they were special, and God's hand was upon little Donovan and Johnathan.

Gabrielle did everything from prayer to spankings, extracurricular activities to constantly shushing their mouths because when it came to their father's rulership, they were willing to take the risk for what they felt was right. Gabrielle would try and intervene as much as possible for the kids from their father's chastisement when it came to trivial matters or honest mistakes. Things like forgetting to remove change from pockets and belts from loopholes before washing clothes or spilling milk on the counter while attempting to fix cereal. *Although they were careful about household chores and their individual*

49

responsibilities, they walked on eggshells to avoid human errors which were inevitable.

Mr. Thomas's discipline was on another level; it was the rage in his eyes, his disappointing facial gestures, the tone in his voice and the cutting words that pierced like a knife. When he was finished, you would feel like a worthless nothing and your world was shattered until you had a chance to recover by proving to daddy that you could do it better the next time. She could see the hurt in her children's eyes and felt their broken little hearts so as a mother, this was extremely hard for her to digest. Many times, Gabrielle would have to wait for her husband to calm down and with a soft tone ask, "Why?" She would often say to her husband "Honey it is not what you do but it is the emotional state you are in when you do it and it is not about what you say but how you say it. *If you can't discipline the kids in love, don't discipline them at all!"*

Children obey your parents because you belong to the Lord, [a] for this is the right thing to do. Honor your father and mother." This is the first commandment with a promise: 3 If you honor your father and mother, "things will go well for you, and you will have a long life on the earth" [b] Fathers, [c] do not provoke your children to anger by the way you treat them. Rather, bring them up with the discipline and instruction that comes from the Lord.

Ephesians 6: 1-4

As time moved on and they grew up, the twins began to shut down during family activities; they were disrespectful to teachers and were over socializing or fighting with peers. Gabrielle knew where the behavioral outburst stemmed from and it was imperative to deal with it at the root cause. After speaking with the twins about their behavior, disciplining them in a firm but loving way and setting counseling sessions for them, she was merciful by deciding not to share this with her husband until the appropriate time. In wisdom, she took into consideration the home environment and the spirit of her husband through asking God for direction about this situation. She knew that it was time for transformation in the Thomas household and understood that to continue like this would not be healthy for the kids mentally, emotionally and spiritually. It was time for a change and if not for herself, for her children!

Pearls of Wisdom

As parents, God has mandated us to teach our children while they are young and to care for their souls. Yes, is it ultimately the responsibility of the man as the head to lead his home, however, it doesn't always work out that way. It's irrelevant whether your husband or father of your kids attend church or not. That has nothing to do with you being a godly example to your children or finding somewhere to fellowship.

So, what do you do as a mother? As a wife? You don't just sit there but you do what you must! Never ignore any mistreatment concerning your kids. Overlooking physical, emotional, mental and even sexual abuse could ultimately hinder your child from becoming a healthy adult in mind, body and spirit, and you will be held accountable! *It is up to you to allow nothing to break your child's spirit.* If this is your situation - seek God on the matter, get spiritual and professional help for your kids. If it continues, you may have to take another route but do something!

Lessons to learn from Gabrielle

Although we understand that discipline is a must in raising a child, it must be done in love. Grandmother who had eleven children of her own told me "When you chastise, correct and discipline your kids they will love and respect you better". A little discipline didn't kill us, and it won't our children. *Those who spare the rod of discipline hate their children. Those who love their children care enough to discipline them."* Proverbs 13:24.

I would rather a spanking than words that would damage a child forever! Speaking life to your children that will encourage them is imperative and especially at a young age. You don't speak negative or allow anyone else to but instead protect them with words of blessings. Declare that their hearts will never become bitter or cold and teach them to be quick to forgive.

You can pray that the love of God finds its way to the heart of your husband and in turn his heart will turn back to his children. Pray that whatever offences, hurts and disappointments that have occurred will not take root in your husbands' life. Denounce the hurt places in his life.

Declare strength and boldness for your journey while never becoming bitter along the way. You are fit and equipped for the master's use!

Thoughts | Reflections | Notes

_____
_____
_____
_____
_____
_____
_____
_____
_____
_____
_____
_____
_____
_____
_____
_____
_____
_____
_____
_____
_____
_____

Susan

"Don't Give Up on Your Desires"

When she was a little girl, Susan and family would go down south every year during the summer months. Her grandmother would have a pantry full of vegetable and fruit preserves and she would send her parents back home with a box full. The canned jars would last the family for months without even being touched because jarred foods have a much longer life expectancy than the average store-bought processed food. Grandma prepared them with lots of love while the foods were still fresh, and the jars weren't opened until it's proper time.

Many years later after several committed relationships, a canceled engagement, and a marriage gone wrong Susan would reminisce back to those memories of grandma. The enemy wanted Susan to keep feeling sorry for herself, abort her dreams and relinquish her desires for marriage over to the enemy. Deep down inside, Susan knew that she was wife material and possessed the selfless character that merited lifelong companionship. She had great examples of virtuous women through her mother and grandmother and she had been studying wifely duties long before her vows were taken. Sadly, she realized that she had acted in a role as wife to those who didn't deserve it! She had given too much of her power over to worthless men. Finally, Susan was content with her status but clear about her desire for marriage. No longer was she anxious or double-minded but sought God for wisdom and discernment while she waited patiently before entering the dating game again.

If any of you lacks wisdom, you should ask God, who gives generously to all without finding fault, and it will be given to you. 6 But when you ask, you must believe and not doubt, because the one who doubts is like a wave of the sea, blown and tossed by the wind. 7 That person should not expect to receive anything from the Lord. 8 Such a person is double-minded and unstable in all of his ways.

James 1:5-8

Pearls of Wisdom

Every thought that you are too old, washed up or it's just too late is just that, A THOUGHT! Remember the importance of walking by Faith and that most answered prayers come with a process. If it is your desire to marry or remarry don't stand down but stand your ground and believe. If marriage was not a realistic possibility, God would not place the desire in your heart!

Delight yourself in the LORD, and he will give you the desires of your heart. Commit your way to the LORD; trust in him, and he will act.

Psalm 37:4-5

Lessons to learn from Susan

While you are waiting for your God ordained husband, never become idle. Building yourself spiritually, mentally, physically and economically will demand higher standards in your mate selection. So, don't settle!

Your past does not define who you are so stop looking back! Be confidently sure of who you are in God for the old woman is dead to Christ. Only forward movement should be your priority while knowing that the best is yet to come.

***No worries, no fretting, no regrets**

"Do not be anxious about anything, but in every situation, by prayer and petition, with thanksgiving, present your requests to God. ⁷And the peace of God, which transcends all understanding, will guard your hearts and your minds in Christ Jesus". Phillipians 4:6-7

Thoughts | Reflections | Notes

_____
_____
_____
_____
_____
_____
_____
_____
_____
_____
_____
_____
_____
_____
_____
_____
_____
_____
_____

In Closing

"Let the Healing Begin"

Although each story may not have been relatable, they are certainly relevant for today because psychological abuse is still very overlooked. It's like a growing cancer in the body that has been confined and never exposed or addressed, and when not confronted it can become hazardous to the mind, body, and spirit. You'll find that most abusers hurt the ones closest to them and they just can't help it. They could very well mistake control for love because that's all they have ever seen or been told. Because of the mental state, idiosyncrasies or just plain pride, families are torn apart, dreams are shattered, and hope is lost. The sad reality is that the victim is always the one pitied but, both the abuser and the abused become damaged goods that essentially must be healed.

A man's spirit will endure sickness, but a crushed spirit who can bear?

Proverbs 18:14

There are many short-term and long-term results of psychological abuse. Shame, anxiety, fear, low self-esteem,

59

depression, withdrawal or thoughts of suicide. Also, as a result of vulnerability or wanting to escape the pain people tend to explore other outlets such as drugs, drinking or falling into the hands of adultery with another lover. No one is exempt from these actions; therefore, healing is imperative to proceed with a productive, healthy and whole life.

If you're a believing wife and can identify with the stories in this book, focus on the happy endings knowing that God has gifted you with the ability to win your husband to Christ. As you are one with your husband, pray for the rhythm of his heartbeat and that God will allow you to feel what he feels. Faith forward believing that change is possible, for an angry abuser can become a loving father and husband. God judges the heart of man and he will never push someone beyond their own will, so your responsibility is to examine your own heart. Make sure your heart is clutter free of any bitterness, hate or any unforgiveness toward your spouse. If you know that it's necessary to separate, before you do, give it everything. Don't get caught up with the outcome, just trust God through the process.

Beloved wife, if you heard from God to stay then trust that he will extend to you grace and strength to endure. Proceed with wisdom and hold on to your promise. Again, I say don't get distracted by how things may appear, just believe.

Whether you stay or leave it is a matter of endurance under pressure. Letting the thoughts of the ending consume you won't add a day to your life and will only add stress. Ultimately, divorce is caused from hardness of one's heart.

"For I know the plans I have for you," declares the LORD, plans to prosper you and not to harm you, plans to give you hope and a future.

Jeremiah 29:11

To my single sisters, don't just settle for what looks good, seems decent or feels comfortable. Remember while dating, in a relationship or even engaged when he gives you a preview of his character, take it for what it is, good or bad. Your DNA is rich because of your heavenly father; therefore, you are the prize! If he's a good God-fearing man work with him unless you're instructed differently. Give it everything you've got and trust God.

Twenty-Five ways to identify exposure to Emotional, Verbal or Mental Abuse

1. Constantly put you downs

2. Extreme criticism

3. Refusing to communicate

4. Very Irrational

5. Ignoring or excluding you

6. Extramarital affairs

7. Flirtatious or provocative with opposite sex

8. Unreasonable jealousy

9. Extreme moodiness

10. Ugly jokes about you

11. Saying "I love you but............."

12. Saying "If you don't ____, I will ____ ."

13. Domination and control

14. Very Egotistical

15. Withdrawal of Affection

16. Guilt tripping on you

17. Isolating you from friends or family

18. Using money as a method of control

19. Continuous calling or texting when you're out of their presence

20. Threats to commit suicide if you leave

21. You constantly walk on eggshells

22. You have a fear of speaking up

23. You let them win the disagreement just to keep peace

24. They humiliate you in presence of others

25. Facial expressions of anger or disappointment toward you

Fifteen reasons why Non-physical abuse should not be taken Lightly

1. Emotional abuse can lead to physical abuse

2. Causes low self esteem

3. Living in constant fear

4. Isolates one's self from others because you feel ashamed or stupid

5. You feel hopeless and in despair

6. You can't make a decision on your own without seeking your spouse's approval

7. You resent your spouse, yourself, or life in itself

8. Very judgmental or analytical of yourself

9. Constant depression or anxiety

10. Could have a nervous mental breakdown

11. Causes sickness in the body

12. You lie often (to yourself and others) to cover up your spouse's behavior

13. You make excuses (to yourself and others) for their actions

14. Effects your work ethic or career

You hold back from being your best just to let them feel good

About the Author

Hairstylist, Entrepreneur and Minister, LaShelle prides herself on serving her clients, both professionally and spiritually. Before she was ordained, her work station was considered as her "Pulpit". A native of Maryland, LaShelle prides herself in serving God and encouraging the broken-hearted. She holds a degree in Business Management and is certified is the Property Manager for her family business Adamsland, LLC which houses many less fortunate in Washington, DC.

After years of serving as a Sunday school teacher, Youth mentor, Prayer warrior and a witness to many, LaShelle was ordained as a minister in 2014 under the leadership of Apostle Wayne A. Green of "Armor of Light Christian Worship Center". She also serves as a prayer leader of "Women of Empowerment & Destiny" an organization which encourages women and men through the power of daily prayer under Min. Wendy Trice.

LaShelle resides in Bowie, MD with family.

About the Publisher

At Vision to Fruition, we are dedicated to helping others bring their personal, business, ministry & nonprofit visions to fruition.

Whether it's as grand as a book you want to write, a business you want to start, a conference or event you want to host, a ministry you want to launch or an organization you want to start; or as small as needing a computer repair, logo design or web design; Vision to Fruition will help you walk through the process and set you up for success! At Vision to Fruition we don't have clients, we have Visionaries. We provide solutions to equip others to pursue their visions & dreams with reckless abandon.

LaKesha L. Williams is the Visionary behind Vision to Fruition's Publishing Division. LaKesha, an acclaimed author, speaker, and minister of the Gospel of Jesus Christ, was born to parents Doris & Cleo Williams in Raleigh, North Carolina in 1983. To know LaKesha is to experience a calming spirit infused with gut-wrenching laughter at unexpected times. She has a passion for giving, which is demonstrated wholeheartedly through her founding of Born Overcomers

Inc. a nonprofit organization & movement dedicated to promoting the belief that we were all Born to Overcome.

LaKesha is the Lead Visionary behind Overcomers HQ, which is dedicated to helping others overcome, thrive & bring their visions to fruition. OHQ is comprised of Born Overcomers Inc., LaKesha L. Williams Ministries, Team Overcomers & Overcomers Bling.

She has authored eight books; including two bestsellers; and is also a featured co-author in Open Your G.I.F.T.S. presented by actress & comedian Kim Coles.

In 2015, LaKesha received the Sista's Inspiring Sista's Phenomenal Woman Award. Since then, she has gone on to become the 2016 Indie Author Legacy Award Recipient in the Author on the Rise category, a 2016 Metro Phenomenal Woman Honoree, a 2017 TDK Publishing Author of the Year nominee & the 2018 iShine Awards winner for Author of the Year.

LaKesha, as a virgin herself, is also an advocate of abstinence, purity & virginity until marriage. Currently, LaKesha resides in Southern Maryland & enjoys serving in the community, fellowshipping with her church family at The Remnant of Hope International Church in Prince Frederick Maryland under the leadership of Pastor Margo Gross and spending time with her family & friends watching movies, sharing stories & creating new memories.

In 2018 we have published seven authors, two of which were Amazon Bestsellers. We would love for you to join our family of Visionaries as well!!!

Learn more here www.vision-fruition.com